The
HEAVENLY
PRESCRIPTION

God's Blueprint For a Balanced Life of Health And Wealth

Ayanna Smitherman

Xulon Press

Xulon Press
555 Winderley Pl, Suite 225
Maitland, FL 32751
407.339.4217
www.xulonpress.com

© 2024 by Ayanna Smitherman

All rights reserved solely by the author. The author guarantees all contents are original and do not infringe upon the legal rights of any other person or work. No part of this book may be reproduced in any form without the permission of the author.

Due to the changing nature of the Internet, if there are any web addresses, links, or URLs included in this manuscript, these may have been altered and may no longer be accessible. The views and opinions shared in this book belong solely to the author and do not necessarily reflect those of the publisher. The publisher therefore disclaims responsibility for the views or opinions expressed within the work.

Unless otherwise indicated, Scripture quotations taken from the Holy Bible, New International Version (NIV). Copyright © 1973, 1978, 1984, 2011 by Biblica, Inc.™. Used by permission. All rights reserved.

Scripture quotations taken from the King James Version (KJV)–public domain.

Paperback ISBN-13: 979-8-86850-341-2
Ebook ISBN-13: 979-8-86850-342-9

The HEAVENLY PRESCRIPTION

DEDICATION

To my beloved children and grandchildren, you are the shining stars that have ignited a fire within me to break free from the generational curse of poverty. With God's grace and your unwavering support, I have embarked on a journey to build generations of wealth. This book is dedicated to you for being my constant inspiration and driving force in this pursuit. May the wisdom shared within these pages guide you to a life of abundance and prosperity, in all aspects, for generations to come.

To all the individuals seeking wisdom and transformation throughout the pages of this book, this dedication is for you. May the words within inspire and empower you to cultivate life-changing habits that bring holistic abundance to your own life, as well as to your families and generations to come.

May you find the guidance and tools necessary to break free from limiting beliefs and embark on a journey of health, wealth, and spiritual prosperity. Know that you have the power of God within you to create a legacy of prosperity that will impact not only your present but also the future of your loved ones.

GOD BLESS

WELCOME!

I'm honored to present to you, "The Heavenly Prescription: God's Blueprint For a Balanced Life of Health and Wealth." Health and wealth play crucial roles in pursuing a fulfilling and meaningful existence. Finding the right path to holistic well-being in today's fast and often unpredictable world can be challenging. How fortunate are we to have a timeless and invaluable resource in the Bible? "Your word is a lamp for my feet, a light on my path" Psalm 119:105 (NIV). The Word of God offers wisdom, divine guidance, and profound insights into physical and financial prosperity. This book aims to explore the knowledge within its pages and unveil the blueprint to live a full, and satisfying life.

Throughout this journey, we will observe what the Bible says about health, wealth, and their correlation. This book intends to help us understand the purpose of our body according to God's plan, and the importance of taking care of it as a form of stewardship. We will delve into how God heals and restores us using the miraculous stories in the Bible to understand how the role of faith and prayer makes all the difference. In this book, we learn that wealth isn't just about money. We will discover the purpose of prosperity revealed in scripture to see that it includes the blessings and favor that come from living according to God's will and extends beyond financial measures.

We will embrace the biblical view of work and how to apply the principles of diligence, excellence, and integrity. We will recognize that our work is not simply for income but a way to find purpose and fulfillment, therefore, finding joy and satisfaction in our endeavors. More importantly, this book will encourage us to trust God, the Provider, and the Sustainer. We will learn that even when life gets rough, we can rely on God's promises and not fear or worry.

The reality is that life has its trials, challenges, and suffering. However, we will discover that even amid adversity, health and wealth can help us remain resilient, and strong, and navigate difficult circumstances to emerge victoriously.

REMINDER:

As we learn about health and wealth from the Bible, let us approach these teachings with an open mind and be ready to put them into practice in our everyday routines. This book will serve as a helpful guide, that shows us how to live a life overflowing with blessings, robust health, and lasting prosperity.

CONTENTS

MythBusters xi
Chapter 1: God's Design For Health 1
Chapter 2: Divine Healing and Restoration 13
Chapter 3: Wealth and Stewardship 25
Chapter 4: God's Blessings and Prosperity 35
Chapter 5: The Role of Work and Diligence 45
Chapter 6: Faith, Trust, and God's Provision 53
Chapter 7: Triumphing Challenges and Trials 59
Conclusion 63
Notes 67
Frequently Asked Questions 73
Thank You 75
About the Author 77
Stay Connected 79

MYTHBUSTERS

To achieve a harmonious life, where health and wealth are balanced and inspired by God, it's crucial to identify and debunk the myths surrounding these concepts listed below. Acquiring a deep understanding needs a balanced approach that considers both the spiritual and practical aspects of our life path.

Myth 1: As a reward for their faith, some believe that following God's blueprint for a balanced life guarantees instant wealth and perfect health.
Myth-buster: Faith is a powerful force but God's plan doesn't promise instant wealth or perfect health. It often involves challenges and personal growth. True wealth, in a spiritual sense, extends beyond material riches, and good health requires care, not just divine intervention.

Myth 2: There is a common misconception that financial success and spiritual values are incompatible. Many believe that the pursuit of wealth is inherently selfish and materialistic.
Myth-buster 2: Contrary to popular belief, money is not inherently evil. Its intentions and actions behind its acquisition and usage define its morality. If wealth is obtained

honestly and used to uplift and impact others positively, it can be a force for good.

Myth 3: There is a mistaken belief that poor health is a result of sin or a lack of faith, which suggests that those who suffer from health problems are spiritually deficient.
Myth-buster: Health issues can affect anyone, regardless of faith or morals. While caring for our bodies, it is also essential to recognize that illness and adversity are naturally part of the human experience and can lead to personal growth and empathy. This understanding aligns with God's plan for humanity, for both physical and spiritual well-being.

Myth 4: Many people believe there is a singular, universally applicable formula within God's blueprint for a well-rounded life, which is commonly accepted.
Myth-buster: The blueprint crafted by God is uniquely personal and flexible. It considers the individual's circumstances, talents, and life purposes. What may be effective for one person may not be suitable for another, and this diversity is completely acceptable in the grand design of God's divine plan for each of our lives.

Myth 5: There is a misconception among some that merely relying on spiritual guidance is sufficient to attain wealth and good health, without the necessity of taking practical actions.
Myth-buster: God's blueprint for a balanced life involves a harmonious blend of faith-driven values and practical, diligent effort. While trusting God is crucial, it should not

be a substitute for wise financial decisions like tithing and saving or maintaining a healthy lifestyle through exercise and a balanced diet.

CHAPTER 1

God's Design For Health

Chapter 1 of the book dives into the connection between spirituality and health and how following God's plan for our health can help us achieve overall well-being in our body, mind, and emotions. This chapter combines ancient wisdom with contemporary insight to help us understand how we can live in a way that aligns with what God intended for our well-being.

1
GOD'S DESIGN FOR HEALTH

I can't think of a better place to start than to recall when Paul describes our bodies as temples of God in 1 Corinthians 6:19-20 (New International Version), "Do you not know that your bodies are the temples of the Holy Spirit, who is in you, whom you have received from God? You are not your own; you were bought at a price. Therefore, honor God with your bodies." In the Old Testament, the temple was where God's presence dwelled, and now, the Holy Spirit resides in the temple known as our bodies. As children of God, our bodies serve as a residence for the holy presence of God, the Holy Spirit, and this privilege gives us an intimate and personal connection with God and a divine presence of comfort, empowerment, and guidance. We were once slaves to sin, but due to the selfless act of Jesus Christ dying on the cross, we have been redeemed at a high cost and belong to God; in sight of this truth, we must live lives that mirror the honor and glory of God.

The Bible urges, "...in view of God's mercy to offer our bodies as a living sacrifice, holy and pleasing to God - this is our true and proper worship" (Romans 12:1). God's good, perfect, and pleasing will is that we present ourselves wholly and holy, for His purposes and glory. God is the all-knowing Creator whose plans for us are rooted in love, purpose, and wisdom. When we offer our entire beings - body, mind, soul, and spirit, we live in a manner that replicates the nature of God and aligns ourselves with His will, which is pleasing to Him. We must value, preserve, and show reverence to our bodies, understanding that they are not just vessels for our desires, but instruments through which we can worship and serve God.

With this gift {**And what an astounding gift it is!**}, we are responsible to honor God by treating our bodies with care and esteem, physically and spiritually. In 2 Corinthians 5:1, the Bible asserts that our bodies contain physical and spiritual beings. "For we know that if the earthly tent we live in is destroyed, we have a building from God, an eternal house in Heaven, not built by human hands." This verse reminds us that while our physical bodies are fleeting and eventually die, our spirits will continue to exist. Since our bodies are a gift from God, we should take good care of them while we still have them.

As children of God, we must uphold the sanctity of our bodies and focus on spiritual growth, so we can experience the fullness of life that God intended for us. Living a life that reflects the honor and glory of God extends beyond refraining from drug and alcohol use. It encompasses avoiding anything that defiles the body, such as gluttony, sexual immorality, and idolatry. Our bodies are fearfully and wonderfully made as mentioned in Psalm 139:14, and we're created in the image of God. We are commanded to love and cherish our physical bodies, yet we should not give in to our fleshly wants. Galatians 5:17 states, "For the desires of the flesh are against the Spirit, and the desires of the Spirit are against the flesh, for these are opposed to each other, to keep you from doing the things you want to do." There is an inherent struggle between our worldly desires and the prompting of the Holy Spirit within us. As believers, we are called to practice restraint and discipline. We can rely on the guidance of the Holy Spirit to help us overcome temptations and conform our behaviors and thoughts to God's will, including intentionally refraining from behaviors and practices harmful to our physical well-being and spiritual growth.

Stewardship is the responsibility of taking care of something entrusted to us. That said, when we accept that our bodies are a precious gift from God, we will understand the importance of conserving and nurturing our emotional, mental, and physical health as an act of worship to God. "So whether you eat or drink or whatever you do, do it all for the glory of God" (1 Corinthians 10:31).

Making choices that intentionally foster holistic well-being honors our bodies as temples of the Holy Spirit and brings glory to God. These actions extend beyond eating or drinking but include all aspects of our lives. We should be mindful of the will of God, how we conduct ourselves, and how we speak and think while striving to reflect His character in whatever we do. In the third chapter of Proverbs (vv. 7-8), Solomon tells his son, "Do not be wise in your own eyes; fear the Lord and shun evil. This will bring health to your body and nourishment to your bones." Through scripture, we learn that knowledge and wisdom require honoring God and obeying His commands. In doing so, we recognize that our bodies and well-being are essential to our existence, and we must approach caring for them with gratitude and respect.

"For physical training is of some value, but godliness has value for all things, holding promise for both the present life and the life to come" (1 Timothy 4:8). Physically, we are required to maintain a healthy lifestyle through being mindful of our overall physical health, including getting sufficient rest, practicing good hygiene, proper nutrition, regular exercise, seeking medical attention as needed, and avoiding harmful substances. Emotional and mental health are also essential elements of stewardship. Participating in activities that promote self-care, such as managing stress, nurturing positive thoughts, personal development, and self-reflection, will ultimately enhance our abilities to carry out obligations and lead fulfilling lives. While emotional, mental, and physical health are major it is in our best interest to cultivate our spiritual health as it will benefit our time on this earth and in eternity.

As humans, we must take good care of our bodies, which are meticulously designed and capable of incredible acts **{I always say they resemble machines that require recurrent maintenance}**.

Our bodies enable us to travel the world, form meaningful connections, pursue our dreams, and realize our purpose. When we treat our bodies as sacred vessels, we acknowledge their importance to our existence.

Stewardship is not just about our bodies. We are responsible for the environment that God created to sustain us. In Genesis 1, God gave us dominion over the earth, and we are to be caretakers of His creation.

All living beings are interconnected, are affected by choices, and yearn for restoration. "For the creation waits eagerly for the children of God to be revealed. For the creation was subjected to frustration, not by its own choice, but by the will of the one who subjected it, in the hope that the creation itself will be liberated from its bondage to decay and brought into freedom and glory of the children of God" (Romans 8:19-21). Biblical principles teach us that we should preserve God's creation. We should make informed choices to safeguard our health and the environment. Prioritizing the sacredness of our physical existence and environmental viability to ensure the welfare of future generations is crucial.

Just as a doctor writes a prescription to help their patients manage or get over specific medical issues and treat their symptoms, there is a timeless blueprint in the Word of God for leading a balanced, healthy life. These principles for diet, exercise, rest, and self-care are not only advantageous for our emotional, mental, and physical well-being, but also develop spiritual wholeness. Let's examine these biblical teachings in more detail.

- **Diet**

As stated earlier in the chapter, we must treat our bodies as temples of the Holy Spirit. Accordingly, the Bible counsels us to make wise choices and consume wholesome food in our diet.

For instance, the Israelites live by specific dietary laws promoting clean and unclean foods, as defined in Leviticus 11 {**Yupp, all 47 verses**}. Fast forward to when Jesus tells His disciples, "...nothing that enters a person from the outside can defile the inside; it doesn't go into their heart, but into the stomach, then out of the body... (In saying this, Jesus declared all foods clean)" (Mark 7:18-19). With that said Christians are no longer bound by those laws. Acts 15:29 does, however, specify dietary restrictions such as meat of strangled animals and sexual immorality, as well as blood and food sacrificed to idols. The verse ends, "You would do well to avoid these things." Fundamentally, we should avoid excesses and harmful substances, as Proverbs 25:16-17 reminds us, it can lead to unfavorable outcomes, teaching the value of restraint and self-control.

- **Exercise**

Besides the previously mentioned 2 Timothy 4:8, the Bible does not mention exercise and fitness per se. Instead, some verses reference dancing (2 Samuel 6:14), hiking (Matthew 14:23), praise and worship (Exodus 15:20), walking (Genesis 5:24), as well as other movements, which could represent the importance of endurance and training. Even though the Bible was written in a pre-fitness era, daily activities in those times were more demanding physically, and required more daily exercise. Through the Word of God, we learn how the care of our bodies through exercise improves our physical health and general well-being, allowing us to serve God and others better.

- **Rest**

Unlike exercise, the topic of rest is found throughout the Old and New Testaments **{Way more}**. Rest is woven into the fabric of creation by God, starting at the beginning when "God finished His work, and rested on the seventh day…and made it holy" (Genesis 2:2-3), so we have the Sabbath. In Psalms 23, David rested in the loving care of the Good Shepherd because he trusted that he was protected and provided for. In another passage, the Lord God says, "Stand at the crossroads and look…ask where the good way is and walk in it, and you will find rest for your souls…" (Jeremiah 6:16) when He is pleading with the Israelites **{who seemingly have lost their way AGAIN}**, to ask questions about taking the best course, and in doing so, they would end up on the right path, where they would find not only bodily rest but a deep, enduring rest for their souls. And who can forget the very well-known Matthew 11:28-30 when Jesus said, "Come to me, all who are weary and burdened, and I will give you rest. Take my yoke upon you and learn from me, for I am gentle and humble, and you will find rest for your souls. For my yoke is easy and my burden is light. There are many more **{I will reference some at the end of the chapter*}**. We can refuel physically, emotionally, and spiritually by resting. It deepens our relationship with God and reminds us to rely on His provision rather than continuously exerting our own might.

- **Self Care**

Once more, self-care is not cited in the Bible verbatim either, but some verses **{Well, at least 33 according to Google}** in the Old and New Testaments allude to the concept. Self-care is the well-being of our bodies, minds, and spirits. God's Word tells us, "Casting all your cares upon Him; for He careth for you" (1 Peter 5:7, King James Version), and one of my personal favorites from the fourth chapter of the Book of Proverbs, "Above all else, guard your heart, for everything you do flows from it" (v. 23, NIV). In Mark 12:31, Jesus teaches us to love our neighbors as ourselves, but we cannot be productive if we do not first care for ourselves. Along with healthy boundaries, encompassing ourselves around positive vibes, exercising forgiveness, managing stress, meditation, and prayer, we must seek out God's peace and presence to facilitate the self-care principles rooted in the Bible to heal our spirits.

The Bible clarifies that our bodies are more than just vessels of the flesh but are also sacred abodes for the Holy Spirit. When we recognize this truth, we should be motivated to treat our bodies respectfully while exercising restraint, purity, and the stewardship God desires. When we follow His blueprint, we not only give God the glory in our bodies but align ourselves with His divine design for holistic well-being and position ourselves for the abundant lives He intended us to live. Stewardship not only frames the care of our bodies as an act of worship and gratitude to God, but we also contribute to the well-being of the world around us. The air we breathe,

the water we drink, and the food we eat all come from the natural world; as a result, our actions affect the environment. Stewardship challenges us to consider the gift of life and to care for it with intent and purpose. These benefit our physical existence and the ecosystem and honor God, who has entrusted them to our care.

* SCRIPTURES THAT REFERENCE 'REST' *

EXODUS 20:8-10	MARK 6:31	PSALM 46:10	PSALM 62:1-2
PSALM 4:8	JOHN 16:33	PSALM 116:7	HEBREWS 4:9-11
JOHN 14:27	PSALM 37:7	EXODUS 33:14	ISAIAH 40:28-31

CHAPTER 2

Divine Healing & Restoration

Chapter 2 is about the incredible power of healing that is part of God's plan and the changes that can come from spiritual renewal. This chapter examines how faith and submitting to God, can affect physical and emotional help. The Bible has examples of those healed by God, and we learn how adhering to His word can bring healing and restoration. The ideas in this chapter are timeless and can help us feel better now and in the future.

2
DIVINE HEALING & RESTORATION

Divine healing is a sign of God's grace and power and is still part of who He is and His plans for us. The Bible has many accounts of miraculous healings that illustrate the depth of God's character and His transformative, healing touch. Divine healing displays God's compassion, love, and sovereignty. Inherently, He wants to heal His children - body, mind, soul, and spirit. In Psalm 103:2-3 David proclaims, "Praise the Lord, my soul, and forget not all His benefits - who forgives all your sins and heals all your diseases.." **{He forgives and heals...Our God is soo awesome}**!

There are countless illustrations of God's divine healing in the scriptures. Early on, God reveals Himself as Jehovah Rapha, when He tells Moses and the Israelites, "... for I am the Lord, who heals you" (Exodus 15:26), expressing a desire to restore and bring wholeness to His people. In times of sickness and trouble, we should confidently seek God's will and restorative touch, trusting Him for divine healing. In response to King Hezekiah's prayers in 2 Kings 20:1-7, God healed him and added fifteen years to his life. Similarly, the Lord told Solomon in 2 Chronicles 7:14 that He would forgive His people of their sins and heal their land if they were humble, pray, and seek His face. In Isaiah, the prophecy said that Jesus would be pierced for our transgressions, crushed for our iniquities, the peace for us would be punishment on Him, "and by His wounds, we are healed" (chapter 53, verse 5), and with that, healing is possible through the sacrifice of Jesus Christ. This serves as a reminder that faith and prayer give us hope in the transformative healing power of God.

The unparalleled healing ministry of Jesus is unveiled in the Gospels of the New Testament. For instance, in Matthew 4:23 Jesus was teaching, proclaiming the good news of the Kingdom, and "healing every disease and sickness among the people." Acts 10:38 aptly describes how "God anointed Jesus of Nazareth with the Holy Spirit and power and He went around doing good and healing all who were under the power of the devil because God was with Him." Whether Jesus traveled around or served the flocks that followed Him, He was healing the blind, the demon-possessed, the lame, and the sick **{This was all before He went to the cross for us}**. After He died and resurrected, Jesus commissioned His disciples to "..place their hands on sick people, and they will get well" (Mark 16:18). This authorization was not only for the disciples but now extends to believers like you and me. James 5 addresses questions such as "Is anyone among you in trouble? **{Trouble isn't just disorder...It includes anxiety, depression, distress, heartache, lack of peace, etc.}** Is anyone among you sick?" It also proposes, "Let them call the church elders to pray over them...And prayer offered in faith will make the sick person well; the Lord will raise them up" (vv. 13-15).

God doesn't change, and His healing power will remain throughout time and sustain all generations. All who believe, have faith and trust in God have access to His healing power. Jesus told His disciples, "...whoever believes in me will do the works I have been doing...I will do whatever you ask in My name, so that the Father may be glorified in the Son" (John 14:12-13). This is the significance of divine healing, and why it is still relevant today.

The healing miracles hold a profound place in the Bible and are supernatural events that beautifully show God's divine treatment of restoring emotional, mental, physical, and spiritual health. They demonstrate His power and compassion for us, give believers hope, and encourage unwavering faith. Let's read and study the relevance of a few notable instances of these healing miracles.

- **The Paralyzed Man** (Mark 2:1-12)

In this popular scripture from the Bible, Jesus forgives and heals a paralytic. What makes this passage all the more astonishing is the faith of the man's friends. Because a great crowd had gathered to hear Jesus preach, the four men couldn't get their paralyzed friend to Him for healing, so they opened the roof and lowered the mat with the immobilized man down to Jesus instead. "When Jesus saw their faith, He said to the paralyzed man, 'Son, your sins are forgiven...I tell you, get up, take up your mat and go home" (vv. 5, 10). The amazing recovery of the paralyzed man's bodily abilities revealed Jesus' divine power over physical and spiritual illnesses and His ability to forgive sins. Jesus addresses both aspects of the man's condition, as there's an inseparable connection between the two.

- **The Blind Man** (John 9:1-12)

These verses tell us that Jesus heals a man born blind. Before the healing process even begins, He points out to His disciples that the man is blind not because of his parent's sins but so that God's work is displayed. Jesus then spits on the ground to make mud, puts it on the man's eyes, and tells him, "Go, wash in the Pool of Siloam (this word means 'Sent'). So the man went and washed, and came home seeing" (v.7). **{The streets (or rather the roads) are talking now…lol}**. The people want to know, "How then are your eyes opened?" and the man responds in so many words, "Jesus put some mud on my eyes, told me to wash, I did, and now I can see" (vv. 10-11). By performing this miracle, Jesus not only gave the blind man his sight back, but He also exemplified the spiritual understanding that results from trusting in Him. It serves as a reminder that Jesus can give us the ability to view things clearly, and from different perspectives. It also highlights the capacity at which Jesus completely changes lives, especially those viewed as hopeless cases.

- **The Woman With an Issue of Blood** (Luke 8:43-48)

Can you imagine having an ailment without relief for many years? This is the case with a woman in the book of Luke. The eighth chapter finds Jesus out and about teaching, telling parables, calming storms, and permitting a legion of demons to leave a man to go into some pigs feeding on the hillside. When Jesus was to be around, there'd usually be a large crowd to welcome Him, and this day was no different. In fact, Jesus was on His way to Jairus's house, where the synagogue leader pleaded for Him to come to heal his dying daughter. As He walked through the crowd, Jesus felt the power had gone out from His body and asked, "Who touched me?" (vv. 45-46). **{I envision the disciples asking each other quietly with a side-eye stare, "Is Master serious right now?"}**. When no one admitted to it, Peter reminded his Rabbi that there was a crowd, and people were pressing against Him. Finally, a woman fell at His feet trembling and confesses that she "had been subject to bleeding for twelve years (she had spent all she had on doctors), but no one could heal her" (v. 43). In an earlier narrative, Matthew 9:21 reads, "She said to herself, 'If I only touch His cloak, I will be healed.'" That's what she did, and she instantly stopped bleeding! Jesus turns to her and responds, "Daughter, your faith has healed you. Go in peace" (v. 48). This healing miracle should make us think of the value of tenacity, faith, and the healing power of touch.

- **The Centurion's Servant** (Matthew 8:5-13)

This passage is so noteworthy because Jesus was not even physically present when He performed this miracle of healing - let's dive deeper. A centurion {**FYI: was a Roman officer; Romans despised the Jews**} approached Jesus and reported that his servant "lies at home paralyzed, suffering terribly" (v. 6). Jesus ready and willing, offered to go heal the servant. However, the centurion feeling unworthy to have Jesus under his roof replies, "But just say the word, and my servant will be healed" (v. 8). The centurion's remarks amazed Jesus! "Truly I tell you, I have not found anyone in Israel with such great faith." He addressed those following Him and continued speaking to the centurion, "Go! Let it be done just as you believed it would" (vv. 10, 13). As indicated, this display of divine authority and power solidifies Jesus's infinite healing abilities and the profound impact of unfaltering faith.

- **Lazarus** (John 11:1-44)

Martha and Mary {Fun fact: This is the Mary that wiped Jesus's feet with perfume and her hair, not Mary his mother} had a brother named Lazarus who laid sick, and Jesus loved all three of them. When He heard His friend was sick, Jesus decided to go back to Judea even though the Jews there tried to stone Him, but not right away. By the time Jesus arrived at the place where the sisters and brother lived, Lazarus had been dead and buried in the tomb for four days. When Martha saw Jesus coming, she went to greet Him, and in her grief decided to tell Him, "Lord, if you had been here, my brother would not have died." (v.21), to which Jesus replied, "Your brother will rise again", and He continued, "I am the resurrection and the life. The one who believes in me will live, even though they die; and whoever lives by believing in me will never die." "Do you believe this?" (vv. 23, 25-26), Jesus asked her as she went back to inform her sister that The Teacher had arrived. Mary reached where Jesus was, and expressed her regret that He wasn't there *before* her brother died. The Bible says that Jesus was "deeply moved in spirit and troubled" (v. 33) when He saw His friends weeping and also wept (v. 35). After being taken to the place where Lazarus lay, Jesus called in a loud voice, "Lazarus, come out!" (v. 43). Jesus demonstrated His authority over death when He raised Lazarus from the dead. This profound miracle was a precursor of Jesus's resurrection, offering hope to Christians that life beyond death is possible, and that physical death is not the end through Him. It also reminds us that God will get the glory even in death.

To experience God's healing power, we must understand the importance of faith, community, and prayer. These components are crucial in establishing a person's relationship with God and supporting their bodily, emotional, and spiritual healing.

In the Bible, faith is frequently mentioned as a crucial element in receiving healing. "Faith is being sure of what we hope for and certain of what we do not see" (Hebrews 11:1). Simply put, faith is completely believing without yet seeing the proof {**I can write a book just on having faith**

alone, but I won't get ahead of myself}. Christianity and faith go hand in hand, and we as believers are encouraged to put our complete faith and assurance in God's power to heal. When experiencing mental, emotional, physical, or spiritual difficulties, faith in God's compassion, mercy, and strength can give us hope and assurance.

Being a part of a community that embraces true faith enables us to unite and provide or receive prayers, encouragement, and comfort in times of need. Jesus said, "Again truly I tell you that if two of you on earth agree about anything they ask for, it will be done for them by my Father in Heaven. For where two or three gather in my name, there am I with them" (Matthew 18:19-20). Collective prayers, support, and help of other Christians can be a source of spiritual and emotional fortitude. Galatians 6:2 reads, "Carry each other's burdens, and in this way, you will fulfill the law of Christ." Being in the presence of compassionate and nurturing people can greatly impact the course of a person's healing. Community plays a vital role and believers should impart edification and accountability to each other, so "therefore confess your sins to each other and pray for each other that you may be healed" (James 5:16a).

Prayer is a means of direct communication between us and God. Through prayer we seek His guidance, healing, intervention, and strength, having confidence in knowing God hears us, has our best interest at heart, and will answer us **{I'm inclined to point out that it may not be what we WANT, but GOD's will is definitely what we NEED}**. 1 John 5:14-15 is a relevant scripture about prayer that reads, "This is the confidence we have in approaching God: that if we ask anything according to His will, He hears us."

It continues, "And if we know that He hears us - whatever we ask - we know that we have what we asked of Him." Another familiar passage of scripture in Philippians chapter four tells us, "Do not be anxious about anything, but in every situation, by prayer and petition, with thanksgiving, present your requests to God. And the peace of God, which transcends all understanding, will guard your hearts and minds in Christ Jesus." (vv. 6-7). Prayer can be individual or communal, either way, we're manifesting our reliance on God for His divine emotional, mental, physical, and spiritual healing while having unwavering faith that it will be done **{I implore you, pray without ceasing}**.

The Old and New Testaments of the Bible contribute to the biblical foundation of divine healing. The fact that God is the healer, that Jesus had a healing ministry, and that healing continued in the early church are all signs that divine healing still occurs today. As Christians, we are urged to accept this reality and look to God for healing, believing His ability to heal and restore is still applicable and available to us today.

The healing miracles in the Bible, serve as powerful testimonies of God's love, mercy, and desire to restore the health and well-being of His people. They remind us that, through faith, we can experience divine healing in all aspects of our lives. The integration of faith, community, and prayer creates a powerful union for Christians who believe it can lead to experiencing God's healing power. While these elements are significant, I will reiterate that healing can be exhibited in various ways, including physical, emotional, and spiritual restoration, and may not always align with our expectations or desires.

CHAPTER 3

Wealth and Stewardship

Chapter 3 will explore how money and our responsibilities as faithful stewards are connected. This chapter teaches us to use our resources wisely, appreciate what we have, and understand why abundance is a part of our divine design.

3
WEALTH AND STEWARDSHIP

{Now we get to the nitty-gritty ... lol}

I have adopted the phrase, "Health is Wealth." It implies that good health is a form of wealth that is invaluable and essential for a balanced life. We usually associate wealth with financial resources and material possessions, but if we do not lead a healthy lifestyle, even the most precious treasures can become meaningless. We have addressed the divinely prescribed instructions for health; let's dive into some biblical concepts for prosperity and how they relate to our actions, obligations, and views concerning fortune and resources. Wealth itself isn't innately ungodly, but how it is obtained, shared, and used is significant.

- "But seek first God's kingdom and righteousness, and all these things will be given to you as well." According to Matthew 6:33, we must prioritize spiritual growth and conform to God's will while trusting that He will provide our earthly needs and things beyond this physical realm.

- The Bible forbids us to love money because it can result in moral and spiritual decline. 1 Timothy 6:10 states, "For the love of money is the root of all kinds of evil. Some people eager for money, have wandered from the faith and pierced themselves with many griefs."
- Money can be a gift from the Lord God. "The blessing of the Lord brings wealth, without painful toil for it" (Proverbs 10:22). True wealth does not come through misery or other unethical means; it comes from God's favor. Proverbs 13:1 warns, "Dishonest money dwindles, but whoever gathers money little by little makes it grow. " If we acquire resources diligently, honestly, and gradually they will be sustained.
- As Christians, we are to be stewards of the resources God has given us. The Bible tells us that to the one much is given, much is required, and to the one who has been entrusted with much, then much more will be asked of them (Luke 12:48). We are responsible for managing wealth, which includes paying tithes, furthering God's kingdom, and blessing others **{My pastor teaches these principles regularly}.** Faithful stewardship is paramount, and there are consequences for neglecting our responsibilities.
- Jesus encourages us to place value in relevant eternal spiritual investments rather than earthly riches. "Do not store up for yourselves treasures on earth…But store up for yourselves treasures in Heaven…For where your treasure is, there your heart will be also" (Matthew 6:19-21). The growth

of material prosperity is fragile and transient. Instead, let us serve God and help others accumulate eternal wealth.
- Scriptures urge the wealthy to remain content and humble. "Keep falsehood and lies far from me; give me neither poverty nor riches, but give me only my daily bread. Otherwise, I may have too much and disown you and say, 'Who is the Lord?' Or I may become poor and steal, and so dishonor the name of my God" (Proverbs 30:8-9). They also advise against placing their trust solely in riches and excessive possessions or materialism.

> 1 Timothy 6:17-19 tells us, "Command those who are rich in this present world not to be arrogant nor to put their hope in wealth, which is so uncertain, but to put their hope in God, who richly provides us with everything for our enjoyment. Command them to do good, to be rich in good deeds, and to be generous and willing to share. In this way, they will lay up treasure for themselves as a firm foundation for the coming age so that they may take hold of the life that is truly life."

These biblical teachings offer insight into the value of using riches to glorify God and bless others while practicing stewardship, integrity, and generosity, a true life fulfillment.

Our blessings are meant to be shared with others, and we are urged to cultivate a spirit of giving. It encourages us to find satisfaction in what we already have rather than always pursuing worldly gain by realizing that true abundance comes from contentment. Additionally, the scriptures encourage us to make intentional and thoughtful financial decisions, teaching us to handle money wisely and reflect God's will in our choices. Here we will look at what the Bible tells us about three tenets of financial stewardship: generosity, contentment, and wise decision-making.

Generosity is a foundational principle of financial stewardship and signifies us giving to others wholeheartedly and willingly.

- (Proverbs 11:24-25) "One person gives freely, yet gains even more; another withholds unduly but comes to poverty. A generous person will prosper; whoever refreshes others will be refreshed."
- (Luke 6:38) "Give, and it will be given to you. A good measure, pressed down, shaken together, and running over, will be poured into your lap. For with the measure you use, it will be measured to you."
- (2 Corinthians 9:6-7) "Remember this: Whoever sows sparingly will also reap sparingly, and whoever sows generously will also reap generously. Each of you should give what you have decided in your heart to give, not reluctantly or under compulsion, for God loves a cheerful giver."

Contentment means that we find fulfillment and peace with what we already have. It helps us avoid the traps of consumption and dissatisfaction.

- (Ecclesiastes 5:10) "Whoever loves money never has enough; whoever loves wealth is never satisfied with their income. This too is meaningless."
- (Philippians 4:11-13) "I am not saying this because I am in need, for I have learned to be content whatever the circumstances. I know what it is to be in need, and I know what it is to have plenty. I have learned the secret of being content in any and every situation, whether well-fed or hungry, whether living in plenty or want. I can do all things through (Christ) who gives me strength."
- (Hebrews 13:5) "Keep your lives free from the love of money and be content with what you have, because God has said, 'Never will I leave you; never will I forsake you'."

Wise decision-making demands that we seek counsel from God and His Word to make wise financial decisions. In this way, we make intentional, mindful choices in managing our resources.

- (Proverbs 3:9-10) "Honor the Lord with your wealth, with the first fruits of all your crops; then your barns will be filled to the overflowing, and your vats will brim over with new wine."

- (Proverbs 6:6-8) "Go to the ant, you sluggard; consider its ways and be wise! It has no commander, no overseer or ruler, yet it stores its provisions in summer and gathers its food at harvest."
- (Proverbs 21:5) "The plans of the diligent lead to profit as surely as haste leads to poverty."

While referring to making wise decisions, I have a bonus; the Bible cautions us against taking on excessive debt in Proverbs 22:7, "The rich rule over the poor, and the borrower is a slave to the lender," and again in Romans 13:8 where it says, "Let no debt remain outstanding, except the continuing debt to love one another, for whoever loves others has fulfilled the law."

We have read many insightful verses in the Bible that call our attention to the moral and spiritual dangers that can surface from a harmful attachment to worldly possessions. Through their teachings, believers are warned not to allow the pursuit of money to overpower their spiritual well-being. Instead, we should embrace and prioritize characteristics like contentment, giving, and a heart set on eternal values.

Throughout the Old and New Testaments, we learn the conflict between serving God and having an unhealthy obsession with money, how our desire for wealth can have negative effects, that acquiring material assets fails to accurately reflect an authentic existence, and how we foolishly look for enduring happiness in riches and materialism. "No one can serve two masters. Either you will hate one and love the other, or you will be devoted to the one and despise the other. You cannot serve both

God and money." Jesus's words in Matthew 6:24 stress dedication to spiritual concerns instead of letting material goals take precedence. Proverbs 11:4 & 28 inform us, "Wealth is worthless in the day of wrath, but righteousness delivers from death. Those who trust in their riches will fall, but the righteous will thrive like a green leaf." These verses capture the theme of trusting God instead of our wealth because money and material possessions will not last. In Luke 12, Jesus is teaching us the need to realize the emptiness of materialism and covetousness as a means of fulfillment when He said, "Watch out! Be on your guard against all kinds of greed; life does not consist in an abundance of possessions" (v. 15).

The overall message emphasizes the proper use of resources to better ourselves and the interests of others while continuing to keep God's purposes and will front and center. Following these principles will help us manage our finances in a way that glorifies God, benefits others, and encourages a pragmatic and ethical attitude to wealth and assets. Understanding the dangers of greed, materialism, and the love of money puts in perspective that allowing these pursuits undermines our spiritual journey and the need to prioritize our eternal values, contentment, and a heart aligned with God's teachings.

CHAPTER 4

God's Blessings and Prosperity

In this chapter, we explore ancient wisdom from the Bible that can change the way we think about blessings and wealth. We dig into the teachings of the scriptures, uncovering key ideas about the true purpose of having wealth, following God's rules, and having faith. These teachings work together to bring us grace and abundance. Through reading interesting passages and thinking about them, we learn crucial lessons that can guide us toward a life filled with blessings and prosperity.

4
GOD'S BLESSINGS AND PROSPERITY

Biblical prosperity goes beyond money and possessions and includes various aspects of well-being, such as emotional, relational, and spiritual, wholeness. While having financial abundance can be a part of this prosperity, the Bible teaches us that true flourishing involves having a strong, intimate relationship with God, living a righteous and generous life, finding contentment, and experiencing healthy relationships and inner peace. When we dive into the teachings of Scripture, we can discover profound wisdom that helps us grasp a more comprehensive notion of prosperity that surpasses mere material wealth.

Revisiting Matthew 6:33 for a second time {This principle is very important}, we are being reminded that in seeking God's kingdom and righteousness, true prosperity starts with our spiritual well-being. It's about having a strong relationship with God, living in a way that pleases Him, and obeying His commands. God will supply our needs and bless us abundantly when we put Him and His will at the center of our lives. Our definition of prosperity should extend beyond material wealth. While God does care about our physical needs, He also desires for us to experience spiritual, emotional, and relational prosperity. When we seek God first, everything else falls into place and we can experience true and lasting prosperity in every aspect of our lives.

Riches refer to more than just material possessions. It implies finding fulfillment in God's presence and cultivating a heart of gratitude towards Him. "But godliness with contentment is great gain. For we brought nothing into this world, and we can take nothing out of it" (1 Timothy 6:6-7). Gratitude is an attitude of appreciating the goodness and provision of God, regardless of what we have or our circumstances. Finding fulfillment in God's presence is the ultimate satisfaction that comes from having a deep relationship with Him. The things of this world may come and go, but the presence and peace of God are constant sources of joy and fulfillment. Prosperity includes our generosity and blessing of others. God honors and increases our acts of kindness, in as much as giving brings glory to Him. "You will be enriched in every way so that you can be generous on every occasion, and through us, your generosity will result in thanksgiving to God. This service that you perform is not only supplying the needs of the Lord's people but is also overflowing in many expressions of thanks to God" (2 Corinthians 9:11-12). God blesses us so that we can bless others, in addition to receiving blessings for ourselves. We show God's provision and love by being generous and meeting other people's needs. This in turn inspires individuals who receive assistance to express gratitude and praise to God for His provision and grace. Giving meets practical needs but has a profound spiritual significance as well.

Prosperity produces an inner peace that comes from trusting God no matter what the circumstances may be {**Trust me I know, that can be super hard to do!**}. God will "keep in peace all whose minds are steadfast because they trust in you" (Isaiah 26:3). God is faithful and to experience contentment, tranquility, and a sense of well-being that goes beyond financial concerns, we must focus our minds on Him and place our trust completely in Him.

The notion of blessings isn't a mere favor, but a complex expression of God's goodness and provision which are frequently met with restrictions that reveal our relationship with God and our adherence to His rules. The circumstances and benefits are described in Scripture, as both are a demonstration of God's faithfulness and the transformative power of His grace.

When we are obedient to God's commands and commit to righteousness, we position ourselves for His favor and fruitfulness. "Blessed is the one who does not walk in step with the wicked or stand in the way that sinners take or sit in the company of mockers, but whose delight is in the law of the Lord, and who meditates on His law day and night. That person is like a tree planted by streams of water, which yields its fruit in season and whose leaf does not wither - whatever they do prospers" (Psalm 1:1-3). Delighting in God's ways and spending time in His word results in a deep-rooted blessing that produces fulfillment and prosperity.

The Bible says, "A generous person will prosper; whoever refreshes others will be refreshed" (Proverbs 11:25). When we are generous in acts of kindness and physical resources, the blessings will flow. The more we contribute to blessing others, the more abundance and renewal we will receive in return.

A humble heart that recognizes the infinite power of God and asks for His guidance is in a position to be elevated and blessed. God will exalt and bless those who are humble enough to acknowledge their need for His grace. If we "humble ourselves before the Lord, He will lift us up" (James 4:10).

The presence of God's appointed benefits and times of refreshing are made possible by repentance. Acts 3:19-20 tells us, "Repent, then, and turn to God, so that your sins may be wiped out, that times of refreshing may come from the Lord, and that he may send the Messiah, who has been appointed for you - even Jesus", reiterating that when we turn away from sin and seek forgiveness, our blessings can be renewed.

From Solomon to Ruth and Paul, we can find encouraging narratives of individuals whose lives manifested the unequivocal touch of God's favor and prosperity throughout the Bible, offering a glimpse of what a deep connection with God can lead to. Let's take a closer look at some of them:

- **Abraham (Genesis 24:1)** "Abraham was now very old, and the Lord had blessed him in every way."

Abraham had faith and was obedient when he left his native land to follow the call of God. This resulted in not only Abraham but his offspring being blessed and prosperous.

- **Solomon (1 Kings 3:10-13)**

"The Lord was pleased that Solomon had asked for this. So God said to him, 'Since you have asked for this and not for long life or wealth for yourself, nor have asked for the death of your enemies but for discernment in administering justice, I will do what you have asked. I will give you a wise and discerning heart so that there will never have been anyone like you, nor will there ever be. Moreover, I will give you what you have not asked for - both wealth and honor - so that in your lifetime you will have no equal among kings.'" **{This gives me goosebumps every time I read it}.**

God granted Solomon unprecedented honor and wealth after he requested wisdom and a desire to serve God's people, instead of the death of enemies, long life, or money.

- **Job (Job 42:12)**

"The Lord blessed the latter part of Job's life more than the former part. He had fourteen thousand sheep, six thousand camels, a thousand yoke of oxen, and a thousand donkeys."

Job displayed unwavering faith and perseverance through very tough times. This brought about a restoration of blessings and prosperity, even exceeding his previous status.

- **Ruth (Ruth 2:11-12)**

"Boaz replied, 'I've been told all about what you have done for your mother-in-law since the death of your husband - how you left your father and mother and your homeland and came to live with a people you did not know before. May the Lord repay you for what you have done. May you be richly rewarded by the Lord, the God of Israel, under whose wings you have come to take refuge.'"

Commitment, kindness, and loyalty led Ruth to the favor of God, and to her eventual inclusion in the lineage of King David and Jesus Christ.

- **Mary (Luke 1:28-30)**

"The angel went to her and said, 'Greetings, you who are highly favored! The Lord is with you.' Mary was greatly troubled by his words and wondered what kind of greeting this might be. But the angel said to her, 'Do not be afraid, Mary; you have found favor with God.'"

Mary was chosen by God to be the mother of Jesus, the Savior of the world. Extraordinary favor was brought upon the mother of the Messiah because of her faith and obedience to God's plan.

- **Zacchaeus (Read Luke 19:1-10)**

"...He wanted to see who Jesus was but because he was short he could not see over the crowd...he ran ahead and climbed a sycamore-fig tree to see Him...When

Jesus reached the spot he looked up and said to him, 'Zacchaeus, come down immediately, I must stay at your house today.' So he came down at once and welcomed Him gladly. All the people saw this and began to mutter, 'He has gone to be the guest of a sinner.' But Zacchaeus stood up and said, 'Look, Lord! Here and now I give half of my possessions to the poor, and if I have cheated anybody out of anything, I will pay back four times the amount.' Jesus said to him, 'Today salvation has come to this house, because this man, too is a son of Abraham. For the Son of Man came to seek and to save the lost.'"

After encountering Jesus, Zacchaeus received salvation. A transformed heart created a complete change in his actions including generosity and making atonement for past infractions.

- **Paul (2 Corinthians 12:9-10)**

"But He said to me, 'My grace is sufficient for you, for my power is made perfect in weakness.' Therefore, I will boast all the more gladly about my weaknesses, so that Christ's power may rest on me. That is why, for Christ's sake, I delight in weaknesses, in insults, in hardships, in persecutions, in difficulties. For when I am weak, then I am strong."

In the face of challenges and weaknesses, the apostle Paul encountered God's favor and fulfillment during his ministry. His dependence on the mercy and grace of God resulted in spiritual abundance and significantly influenced the spread of the Gospel.

Having a lot of money can make us prosperous but to truly experience the kind of wealth that God wants for us, we need to understand and practice being content with what we have, sharing with others, finding peace inside ourselves, and growing spiritually. The Bible teaches us that blessings come when we combine God's incredible kindness with our willingness to follow His rules. If we want God's blessings in our lives, we have to be in sync with His plans, which means having faith, being generous, staying humble, obeying Him, and seeking forgiveness when we make mistakes. When we seek to honor and serve God and live a good life, that's when His favor and prosperity come. While fulfillment may appear in various forms, it ultimately stems from having a strong connection with God and being eager to heed His instructions.

CHAPTER 5

The Role of Work and Diligence

Chapter 5 talks about how important it is to work hard and be diligent, especially from a biblical perspective. The chapter emphasizes how having a purposeful job and feeling personally fulfilled can lead to experiencing God's blessings, which all work together positively. By dedicating ourselves and putting in effort, we can achieve great things and receive many benefits.

5
THE ROLE OF WORK AND DILIGENCE

Putting in effort and work is a fundamental part of being human. The Bible teaches us that working hard is not just about getting things done. It's a way to show respect to God, take care of our duties, and make the world a better place. Parables and other teachings in the Bible show us that working diligently, being honest, and doing our best in whatever we do are important; it's personal growth, taking care of ourselves, and spreading goodness to those around us.

According to the Bible, work is more than a way to make money. It's a multifaceted endeavor that serves as a way to provide and as a source of personal fulfillment and spiritual significance. God loves His creation. The scriptures remind us that we are made in God's image and He has entrusted us with stewardship over the earth. This perspective stresses the value of justly reaping the fruits of our labor and finding purpose through contributing to the well-being of others by working diligently. Let's view labor as a means of provision and gratification from a biblical standpoint.

- Provision Through Work

After Adam and Eve sinned, God told Adam, "By the sweat of your brow you will eat your food until you return to the ground, since from it you were taken; for dust you are and to dust you will return" (Genesis 3: 19), specifying that we are to work for our provision.

- **Stewardship and Blessing**

God's command to Adam and Eve in Genesis 1:28 is to "Be fruitful and increase in number; fill the earth and subdue it. Rule over the fish in the sea, birds in the sky, and over every living creature on the ground." The idea of stewardship and productive labor reflected in this verse is that work is viewed as a way for us to manage and multiply God's creation.

- **Diligence and Prosperity**

The book of Proverbs is well-stocked with wisdom. For example, chapter 10 v. 4 teaches us, "Lazy hands make for poverty, but diligent hands bring wealth." Here we learn the connection between diligence, hard work, and prosperity, making it clear that if we put effort into our work, it leads to provision as well as blessings.

- **The Example of Paul**

"You yourselves know that these hands of mine have supplied my own needs and the needs of my companions.

In everything I did, I showed you that by this kind of hard work, we must help the weak, remembering the words of the Lord Jesus Himself said: 'It is more blessed to give than to receive.'" Paul's example of work in Acts 20:34-35 is deemed to be for the generosity and support of others, in addition to our own provision.

- **Work As a Service to God**

The idea of Colossians 3:23-24 is, "Whatever you do, work at it with all your heart, as working for the Lord, not for human masters." When we labor with commitment and sincerity, "it is the Lord Christ you are serving." It also gives way to a sense of achievement, a source of providing, and "you will receive an inheritance from the Lord as a reward."

- **Finding Joy in Work**

Work is "the gift from God" and therefore we should find the potential for contentment and pleasure of engaging "in all their toil" (Ecclesiastes 3:13).

As we continue in this subject matter of work and diligence, we need to be mindful even of our jobs. Whether we have an employer or are self-employed, the Bible encourages us to perform our duties competently and thoroughly, pursuing excellence. We should also be honest and make ethical decisions. It isn't just about the job itself, through our efforts we honor God and improve the quality of life around us.

The dictionary definition of diligence is careful and persistent work or effort. The biblical definition is making an effort while maintaining trust and reliance on God. Proverbs 13:4 advises us on being lazy saying, "A sluggard's appetite is never filled, but the desires of the diligent are fully satisfied." Diligence aligned with faith ensures spiritual success. Excellence is being exceptionally good in whatever a person does. Early on we've gained an understanding from the Bible that we should do everything as if we're doing it for God's glory (1 Corinthians 10: 31; Colossians 3:23). We please God when we do "everything in a fitting and orderly way" (1 Corinthians 14:40), it is evidence of the greatness He created us to be. Another key characteristic that plays a role in how we work is integrity. "The integrity of the upright guides them, but the unfaithful are destroyed by their duplicity" (Proverbs 11:3). The scripture teaches us to always be sincere and fair in our interactions. This holds even when no one is standing over us watching.

Finding purpose and satisfaction in work through God's calling means understanding that our employment has a higher meaning in that they are a part of God's plan for our lives. It's about recognizing that the work we do is an opportunity to use our unique talents and abilities to make a positive impact on the world, and not just to make a living. By aligning our work with God's calling, we can find deep fulfillment and a sense of purpose in the work we do every day.

Isn't it awesome that God has a special plan for each one of our lives, even down to employment? "For I know the plans I have for you, declares the Lord, plans to prosper you and not to harm you, plans to give you hope and a future" (Jeremiah 29:11). God's calling on your life is a distinct job He has in mind just for you. When we follow God's calling, our work is more meaningful, even ordinary tasks take on a new significance when we do them for God. When our work aligns with God's plan, it can lead to feelings of fulfillment. Proverbs 16:3 tells us, "Commit to the Lord whatever you do, and He will establish your plans." Trusting God with our work can result in success and achievement. God bestows talents and skills on each of us and we, "should use whatever gift has been received to serve others, as faithful stewards of God's grace in its various forms" (1 Peter 4:10). Scripture implies that through our work we should "let your light shine before others", so we can make a positive impact on the world, "that they may see your good deeds and glorify your Father in Heaven" (Matthew 5:16). When we do good work we glorify God and promote goodness to others.

Work is designed to meet physical needs and also to offer a sense of purpose, stewardship, and a means to contribute positively to the world while honoring God. When we work, we should put in the effort, give it our all, and be honest. This goes beyond just doing a job; it's about honoring God, being accountable, and improving the world through our actions. Understanding God's calling is His special plan for us, we will find purpose and satisfaction in work. When we apply that plan along with our skills to our work, it brings a deep sense of meaning, and happiness, while making a positive difference in the world.

CHAPTER 6

Faith, Trust, and God's Provisions

We are about to dig deeper into the intriguing topics of faith, trust, and how they relate to the way we believe in God's support in Chapter 6. We'll continue to discuss ideas of having confidence and belief even when things are uncertain, and how this connects to our understanding of God's guidance and care. Get ready to uncover more of the inspiring ways our faith and trust play a crucial role in our relationship with our Divine Creator and the provisions we experience in our lives.

6

FAITH, TRUST, AND GOD'S PROVISIONS

Our beliefs and attitudes can influence our health and financial situations, therefore, we must develop a faith-driven, positive outlook on our well-being and prosperity. Throughout this book, we have been exploring how different principles including faith can mold the way we approach both the health and wealth aspects of our lives. Let's continue to uncover how developing our faith in God might enhance our sense of general abundance and vitality.

The Bible offers wisdom about excessive worry by encouraging us not to "be anxious about anything, but in every situation, by prayer and petition, with thanksgiving, present your requests to God" (Philippians 4:6-7). We should address challenges with prayer and gratitude. If we just trust God with our concerns it can bring peace that guards our hearts and minds, positively impacting our health and well-being. We cultivate our perspective on faith by giving and trusting God with our finances. Malachi 3:10 strongly suggests that we "bring the whole tithe into the storehouse, that there may be food in my house. Test me in this and see if I will not throw open the floodgates of Heaven and pour out so much blessing that there will not be room enough to store it." Faithfully contributing what rightfully belongs to God acknowledges His provision, and in return, we open ourselves to receiving blessings beyond measure {**In my singing voice, "There will be blessings on blessings"**}! Of course, we put God's ways and principles first above anything else. He promises to provide for our needs and wants when we seek His kingdom and righteousness. Contentment and gratitude regardless of our circumstances, promote faith. We should "give thanks in all circumstances; for this is God's will for you in Christ Jesus" (1 Thessalonians 5:18). A more positive and balanced perspective on health and wealth stems from learning to be grateful for what we have and trusting in God's provision. Trusting in God's unwavering care and seeing Him as the ultimate provider of everything we need is a powerful theme in the Bible. We'll explore how having God as our provider and sustainer might change how we see the blessings and challenges of life while discovering the deep peace that results from putting our faith in His guidance and provision.

How awesome to know that as long as we trust God, we can rest assured that He will provide for all our needs, and we'll lack for nothing. The familiar verse in Psalms 23 tells us "The Lord is my shepherd; I shall not want" (v. 1), and we're reminded that God takes care of us just as a shepherd cares for his flock of sheep. In Matthew chapter 6, Jesus teaches that we should trust in God's provision and let go of anxiety when He says, "Therefore I tell you, do not worry about your life, what you will eat or drink; or about your body, what you will wear. Is not life more than food and the body more than clothes? Look at the birds of the air; do they not sow or reap or store away in barns, and yet your Heavenly Father feeds them. Are you not much more valuable than they?" (vv. 25-26). Jesus points out that if God cares for even the small creatures, He most certainly will provide for us, His cherished ones. We have a wealth of resources at our disposal, and God promises to supply all of our needs that is, what is truly necessary for our well-being when we put our total trust in Him. "And my God will meet all your needs according to the riches of His glory in Jesus Christ" (Philippians 4:19). All we have to do is, "trust in the Lord with all your heart and lean not on your own understanding; in all your ways acknowledge Him, and He will make your paths straight" (Proverbs 3:5-6). If we believe that God knows what we need in every aspect of our lives, we will put all of our trust in His guidance and wisdom. He promises to direct us toward the best decisions and paths for our lives when we involve Him in everything we do and ask for His guidance. In essence, it's about relying on God and having faith that He will guide us.

Surely life's uncertainties can have us in the grip of anxiety, fear, and worry, which is why we should embrace the reassuring promises of God. Trusting in God's promises can provide us comfort and strength, enabling us to escape the clutches of anxiety. A steadfast faith in God's promises can give us a renewed sense of courage and hope to confront the challenges we face.

It is human nature to experience anxiety, worry, and fear. A simple but effective verse, "When I am afraid, I put my trust in you" (Psalm 56:3), reminds us that if we turn to and trust in God, He can help us overcome all of those feelings. Fear, anxiety, and worry are not of God. 2 Timothy 1:7 tells us, "For the Spirit God gave us does not make us timid, but gives us power, love, and self-discipline." We can rely on God's might to help us overcome those spirits that are not of Him. God is constantly with us and grants us encouragement saying, "So do not fear, for I am with you; do not be dismayed, for I am your God. I will strengthen you and help you; I will uphold you with my righteous right hand" (Isaiah 41:10). His presence and support enable us to deal with our fears and anxieties in confidence. David said, "I sought the Lord, and He answered me" showing us that actively seeking God prompts action from Him. He "delivered me from all my fears" (Psalm 34:4). We can find peace and escape from anxiety by turning to God.

The Bible exhorts us to approach our health and prosperity based on faith, trust, and gratitude, realizing that God's provision and direction are essential to having a balanced life. It's crucial to put our needs and well-being in God's hands. We can have a deep feeling of guidance, peace, and security in our life, as we rely on Him as our ultimate provider and sustainer. God promises to help us find comfort from anxiety, fear, and worry. We can feel a sense of calm and strength that enables us to face life's problems with assurance and hope by placing our faith in His promises.

CHAPTER 7

Triumphing Over Challenges and Trials

It's a part of our life's journey to experience and overcome challenges and hardships. Often, we're presented with obstacles in life that put our faith, fortitude, and resiliency to the test. In this chapter, we learn that God allows our suffering to serve a purpose. We examine how adopting a positive outlook and depending on God's divine power can strengthen and help us get through even the most trying situations. Through the timeless wisdom of the Bible, we uncover practical strategies that equip us to navigate life's storms while establishing a deeper connection with God and taking on triumph over adversity.

7
TRIUMPHING OVER CHALLENGES AND TRIALS

It's not always smooth sailing in life but while on this Christian journey, we will have to confront challenges and rough patches head-on. The truth of the matter is that God uses suffering to evolve us into better people, to make us more like Him. These trials may be painful, but they reveal our weaknesses, build character, strengthen, and mature us. Moreover, we must learn that even in the most difficult situations, when we put our faith and trust in God, He can bring us through anything.

We develop character and spiritual growth as a result of suffering. Just as a weightlifter builds muscle strength by lifting weights, overcoming obstacles makes our faith and resilience stronger. Paul said it best in Romans 5:3-5, "Not only so, but we also glory in our sufferings, because we know that suffering produces perseverance; perseverance, character; and character, hope. And hope does not put us to shame, because God's love has been poured out into our hearts through the Holy Spirit, who has been given to us." Suffering yields growth in character and hope.

Just as fire purifies gold, we can grow in faith by facing our adversities {**Are you catching the analogies though?... Lol**}. "Consider it pure joy, my brothers and sisters, whenever you face trials of many kinds because you know that the testing of your faith produces perseverance. Let perseverance finish its work so that you may be mature and complete, not lacking anything" (James 1:2-4). Let us be encouraged to let suffering and trials serve as opportunities for maturity and perseverance because they are not in vain neither are they "worth comparing with the glory that will be revealed in us" according to Romans 8:18; the splendor that lies ahead outweighs them!

In times of trials and tribulations, we can rely on our faith in God, trusting in His grace and power. We who are children of God can have hope and assurance that He "works for the good of those who love Him and have been called according to His purpose" (Romans 8:28). It's important that we avoid complaining and give thanks in all situations because God ultimately has a purpose for everything.

When life throws hurdles at us, what two important matters are at play? {**Hint: You've been reading about them throughout this book**}. You guessed it - health and wealth play a role in navigating difficult circumstances. When we take care of our body, mind, and spirits while being financially secure, we're more capable of handling challenging circumstances. In addition to prioritizing our health and being good stewards of our resources, we must align our thinking with God's plan for our lives. The two things we must have to answer God's call on our lives are a body and mind inclined to move forward and further His Kingdom, as well as the means to create the conditions necessary for His promises to be fulfilled.

At the beginning of the book, I stated that our bodies are temples of the Holy Spirit (1 Corinthians 6:19-20) and the importance of caring for not only our physical but our mental and spiritual well-being also. Luke 2:52 says, "Jesus grew in wisdom and stature and favor with God and man" and Daniel 1:20 reads, "In every matter of wisdom and understanding about which the king questioned them, he found them ten times better than all the magicians and enchanters in his whole kingdom", both passages remind us that holistic wellness is a healthy body and considers other factors such as a sound frame of mind and a deep spiritual connection with God, allowing us to handle obstacles better. The same holds for our resources - when we have a safety net, it's comparable to having a sturdy rope to cling onto during a storm. The Bible teaches us that the wise, "store up choice food and olive oil, but fools gulp theirs down" (Proverbs 21:20). We must be economically astute so that when times get tough, we can feel less stressed and more secure.

We must set goals that are in line with God's word since this is the only guaranteed way we will be in alignment with His promises. God warns us in Deuteronomy 8:18 to remember that He "gives us the ability to produce wealth, and so confirms His covenant" so we must pray, be faithful, and be obedient to stay on the path of blessings and good health.

While we navigate through difficult circumstances, it's all about giving ourselves the best opportunity to manage and emerge better after them. Having good mental, physical, and spiritual health, as well as being smart with our resources can help us overcome obstacles and continue forward-moving with assurance. Similar to a journey, trusting in God's directions, taking care of ourselves, and being organized can go a long way.

> **"Beloved, I pray that you may prosper in all things and be in health, just as your soul prospers"**
>
> **(3 John 1:2 NKJV).**

CONCLUSION

There is a connection between our physical health, spiritual well-being, and wealth. True prosperity results from having a healthy body and a personal relationship with God, in addition to having material possessions. Let's briefly recap the key biblical principles of health and wealth.

The Bible teaches that our bodies are a precious gift from God, so we must care for them properly. It involves nourishing ourselves with healthy food, staying physically active, and avoiding habits that harm our well-being. Through scripture we learned the importance of balance, allowing us to enjoy the good things in life while practicing moderation. This principle extends to all aspects of our lives, including our choices regarding food, and drinks, and managing our finances. Sharing our wealth with those in need is a core principle in the Bible. When we help others, not only do we improve their lives, but we also experience a deep sense of fulfillment and blessing ourselves. The Bible encourages us to prioritize things that hold eternal value, such as love, kindness, and building meaningful relationships, rather than fixating on accumulating wealth and possessions. Let us be encouraged to trust in God and find contentment with what we have and not become consumed by pursuing wealth at the expense of our well-being. While it is acceptable to strive for excellence, we should not let the pursuit of wealth overshadow our overall health and happiness.

Now that we understand them better, let's discuss how we might apply these crucial biblical teachings on health and wealth.

- **Healthy Habits**

Establish healthy habits to take care of our bodies. We can do this by eating well, staying active, and avoiding things that can harm us so we can have more energy and enjoy life to the fullest.

- **Balance**

Balance is the key that helps us enjoy the good things without going overboard. Moderation keeps things in check, whether it's treating ourselves to something special or controlling our spending.

- **Helping Hand**

Jesus said that it's better to give than to receive. Whether we are helping others in need or donating to a charity, these acts of kindness bring us a sense of happiness.

Conclusion

- **What Matters Most**

Real happiness comes from focusing on things like love, kindness, and relationships. While having aspirations of prosperity is appropriate, prioritizing these goals that hold eternal value enables us to live meaningful lives.

- **Trust the Journey**

Having faith that God will work it out and finding contentment in where we are can reduce stress and make life more peaceful. We can strive to achieve our goals while also being grateful in the present.

Positive changes can result from incorporating these biblical concepts into our daily lives. We can ask God for His wisdom to develop healthy habits, find a good balance between our spending and living, reach out to help others, manage our priorities, cultivate contentment, and trust in Him. In doing so, we not only enhance our own lives but also help to create a more compassionate and peaceful world.

Focusing on a holistic nature of well-being means that our overall health and happiness are interconnected. It's not just about physical health, but also about our mental, emotional, and spiritual well-being. Taking care of ourselves involves nourishing our bodies with healthy food, staying active, and avoiding harmful habits. We need to take care of our bodies, control our emotions, be kind to others, nurture relationships, find purpose, and maintain balance to be truly happy and healthy. A balanced approach means finding a middle ground, not going to extremes. It's about enjoying the good things in life while also prioritizing what truly matters, like contentment, faith, goodwill, and love.

In conclusion, every area of our lives plays a part in how we feel overall. When each area is taken care of, they work well together and create a beautiful image of what a fulfilling, wholesome life looks like.

NOTES

The Heavenly Prescription

Notes

The Heavenly Prescription

Notes

The Heavenly Prescription

FREQUENTLY ASKED QUESTIONS

Here are a few FAQs readers may have about "The Heavenly Prescription: God's Blueprint for a Balanced Life of Health and Wealth."

Q: What is the connection between a balanced, healthy life and spirituality?

A: Our bodies are temples for the Holy Spirit, and when we live balanced, healthy lives, we worship God in our bodies and spirits.

Q: How does faith contribute to financial success?

A: Money can be a blessing or a great ruin, depending on how we steward it. Faith can impart the values and way of thinking required for ethical and disciplined money management.

Q: How do meditation and prayer impact mental health and wellness?

A: When we meditate on God's word and pray we are building an intimate relationship with Him, which reduces anxiety, depression, fear, and stress, as well as produces optimism and positivity.

Q: What are the biblical principles for financial stewardship?

A: The Bible tells us that financial stewardship includes prioritizing God by giving Him first through tithes and offerings, avoiding debt, being generous, and budgeting.

Q: Can forgiveness contribute to physical health?

A: Forgiveness is not only a spiritual discipline but also good for our health because holding onto resentment can be harmful to our well-being.

Q: How do we find God's purpose for our lives?

A: We must seek God for wisdom and His direction by reading the Bible and praying, which offers valuable insight into finding our purpose.

Q: How do I maintain a healthy lifestyle in a busy, modern world?

A: Besides building an intimate, personal relationship with God, you must prioritize self-care by balancing work and rest, exercise, and maintaining a healthy diet.

THANK YOU

Readers,

My heart brims with appreciation as I type these words of gratitude for your decision to embark on this journey with me through the pages of "The Heavenly Prescription: God's Blueprint For a Balanced Life of Health and Wealth."

First and foremost, I am humbled and deeply thankful to the Almighty, the divine architect of all wisdom and prosperity. Through God's grace and guidance, this book has come to fruition, serving as a beacon of light for those seeking holistic abundance.

To you, cherished reader, my gratitude is beyond measure. Your trust in this work, willingness to explore its teachings, and dedication to personal growth inspire me more than you know. Your presence on this journey fills each page with purpose and meaning.

To those who have contributed to the creation of this book and shaped its form, to the family and friends who offered unwavering support and encouragement along the way, our collective efforts have transformed a mere idea into a tangible reality, a testament to the power of collaboration and community.

It is my prayer that in the pages of "The Heavenly Prescription," you find solace in its words, guidance in its teachings, and inspiration in its message. May it serve as a steadfast companion on your path to a life of abundance, both in health and wealth.

Once again, thank you, and together, let us embrace the blessings that await us as we walk hand in hand with faith and purpose.

With sincerest gratitude,

Ayanna Smitherman

ABOUT THE AUTHOR

"Giving Honor to God - my Heavenly Father, and the Head of my life. From Him, through Him, for Him are all things, and to Him be glory forever!"

I'm a Christian Life Coach with 25+ years of experience in personal and professional life. I'm passionate about educating, empowering, and serving families and individuals to help them achieve prosperity in every area of life - health, wealth, spiritual, and relational well-being. My unwavering faith is at the core of everything I do, and I aim to inspire others through the same spiritual principles that guide my life. My comprehensive knowledge and dedication pave the path towards a balanced, fulfilling life with my first book, "The Heavenly Prescription: God's Blueprint for a Balanced Life of Health and Wealth." This book is a testament to my commitment to helping others achieve total wellness and financial success through spiritual truths. Join me on this transformative journey and unlock the keys to a more fulfilling and prosperous life.

-Ayanna Smitherman

STAY CONNECTED

Let's keep the conversation going beyond these pages!

    Shoot me an email, text, or DM so you can stay connected with me for updates and insights.

    Your thoughts and feedback are not only welcome but highly anticipated.

    Let's venture on this journey together where the dialogue never has to end.

(347) 460-4327

coachayanna@classicqueens.org

instagram.com/ayannasmitherman

facebook.com/AyannaSmitherman

Milton Keynes UK
Ingram Content Group UK Ltd.
UKHW050157031224
451865UK00019B/213